# in your face publishing

Copyright © 2011 by Jodi Ambrose

First in your face print edition November 2011

Second print edition January 2016

Cover art by Jodi Ambrose

Photography by Jodi Ambrose

Design by Jodi Ambrose

Manufactured in the United States of America

ISBN: 978-0615537115

**www.jodiambrose.com**

**www.jodiambroseblog.com**

**@jodiambrose**

This is dedicated to the love of my life.
You are my greatest blessing, darling Grant.
You took me from darkness to light
and for that I will love you always.

This is also dedicated to my sweet Mommy,
who taught me common sense
and let me know every day that
my thoughts and feelings have value.

# Praise for Jodi Ambrose's Relationship Books

"When it comes to starting a playful yet important conversation about sex and intimacy there's no need to go any further than books by Jodi Ambrose. Writing with both women and men in mind she covers all the bases of what it takes to develop the kind of relationship you want."
–Cyrus Webb, host of Conversations LIVE/Editor-In-Chief of Conversations Magazine


"Jodi Ambrose's books should be required reading for every clueless man and woman who does not understand what can make their relationships "click". Her books are not about blindly going along with what your partner thinks is right. Instead, Jodi Ambrose shows you simple ways to easily get in harmony with your loved one."
–Joey Pinkney, Award-winning Book Reviewer and Author


"Jodi Ambrose reestablishes a connection between oft-mystified partners by revealing emotional necessities integral to the understanding of the differing sexes. Remarkable in their accessibility, both books avoid jargon in favor of practical-living advice. These books won't do the work for you, but they will give you the tools to get the job done yourself."
–Philip Rosenberg, Host of Sex and Politics Radio


"*Sex: How to Get More of It* is a much-needed idiot's guide to women. It is honest, frank, and funny. I wish more books on relationships were this straight-forward and witty. Jodi Ambrose gives practical, real-world advice without sounding preachy or patronizing. I have recommended this book to many men and women as I believe both genders will enjoy and learn a great deal from it."

–Rachel Tighe, Ph.D., Chair, Department of Communication Studies, The University of Virginia's College at Wise

# Acclaim for Jodi Ambrose's Darn Good Eats Cookbook

"This cookbook is a must have. It's not your typical cookbook. Most cookbooks are dull...they give you a recipe and blah blah blah. But with Jodi's witty humor and writing style, this cookbook becomes so much more. Who would think that a cookbook could make you laugh? But it does!

This cookbook is split into parts, which makes it nice and easy. The fact that there are complex meals (for creative people) and simple fixes (for reluctant cooks) is a bonus and pretty much guarantees that there's something in here for everyone. I definitely recommend giving this book a try. I don't think any other author could have figured out a way to make a cookbook funny. Informative and entertaining...WIN WIN!"
–Happy reader

"This is a great cookbook whether or not you like to cook. There are three things about it that make it stand out from other cookbooks:

1. It's divided into two sections: one with more advanced recipes, the second with tasty but less difficult options. As long as you enjoy cooking, nothing in the "advanced" section will be too hard, but everything sounds delicious. If you don't like cooking, or if you have no experience, the "easy" section of the book has low-maintenance recipes (sometimes including pre-packaged ingredients to speed the process). In both sections the directions are very clear - since they were written by someone who doesn't like to cook, the directions are fairly idiot-proof!

2. It comes in black and white and full-color versions so you can buy it whatever your budget is - I think that's awesome!

3. Every recipe is accompanied by a little story about the food - I sat down and read this book cover to cover. Jodi is so funny, and it's very enjoyable to just read the anecdotes about the food - and then there are recipes! It's pretty great."
   –Another happy reader

# Intimacy: How to Get More of It

## A peek into understanding the male mind

## Introduction

Man-brain: a dark and confusing place to which there is no decoder ring. Were it only so easy, right? If only we girls had some simple way of getting into their heads so we could better understand the annoying mystery that is the man-brain. Well, I can't ship you a magic decoder ring for $6.95, but I can offer you some insight into that strange and bewildering place.

First things first. Do you want more intimacy and happiness in your relationship? If you do, you are in the right spot. My goal is to give you some tips and tricks to love and happiness that you can use with your man to get you closer to having the kind of relationship you want.

Keep in mind that much like us girls, who are as different from one another as delicate winter snowflakes, men too cannot all be lumped together. Some men will respond one way, some men will respond another. As such, in this book I'm addressing the "typical" guy, if there is such a thing. I've spoken with myriad men over the years regarding everything you'll read here, so know that my experience with men of all types is what leads me to the suggestions you'll soon read.

We're going to dish about everything from girl parts and boy parts, to sneaky manipulation (wow, that sounds bad!), to swallowing a little bit of pride, to learning how to trust. Remember, my goal is to help you learn the tricks of the trade that will make both you and your man happier.

So, while this book may sometimes seem like a "20 ways to please your man" list, in all sincerity it's about **YOU** being happier in the long run. Believe me when I say that a happy man will do things for you that an unhappy man would sooner jump into a river of acid than do.

In case you are wondering who this book is for, I've designed it for *all* of the ladies, regardless of your relationship status.

- If you aren't currently in a relationship, that's okay. This will teach you what to do once you are in one and may very well help you find a great relationship.

- If you are in a new relationship, this can help you set the pattern for the long haul.

- If you've been around the block with your man and sometimes you just want him to die slowly, this will give you all the tips you need to get it back to being good.

- Last but not least, even if you are in the most amazing relationship on earth and think that God grew your man in a pod, just for you, you'll still likely learn a few things that can enhance even your wonderful relationship.

But before we jump into this, I just have to lay a few things out on the table. If you are in a relatively new relationship and you've had that "come to God" moment when you realized that your man is just a total insufferable asshat, might I suggest IMMEDIATELY running for the hills, especially before everything is complicated with babies and houses and joint savings accounts. I can't help you if you like men who treat you like shit (as much as I'd like to).

If you are in a long-term relationship, especially one with children, I understand that it is significantly more difficult to run screaming into the night. If you do decide to stick it out, for whatever reason, and follow some of the items on **THE LIST**, you should see some improvement in his behavior. He may not be the man you dreamed of as a girl, but he may certainly be a damn sight better than he has been.

Ultimately, I wish you much love and happiness in your relationship. I've created **THE LIST** after speaking with many men and truly listening to their biggest complaints. I hope that you are able to adapt the items on **THE LIST** to your own life and that each day is happier than the last. Good luck!

## THE LIST

1.  Potty-time is private time

2.  Act like your man is your hero, your knight on a steed, your Prince Charming, blah blah blah...

3.  Compliment his one-eyed trouser snake

4.  Try to avoid being a controlling lunatic

5.  Keep your muff issues to yourself

6.  Let him relax when he gets home from work

7.  Always remember that men are visual creatures

8.  Try something new in the bedroom

9.  Be very clear about what pisses you off and what makes you happy

10. Quit saying, "Nothing" when asked, "What's wrong?"

11. Your muff is not a weapon

12. Turn off the bitch factor

13. Fulfill most of his "Woman Checklist"

14. Being a nag is a no-no

15. Talking during the game is taboo

16. Stay the hell out of his phone and computer

17. Fight in a fair and constructive way

18. Avoid asking him, "What are you thinking?"

19. Live by the $10^5$ rule

20. If you are PMSing or having your girl-time, suck it up

If you are thinking to yourself, "Good grief! She's asking me to be a saint!" no need to worry, as I promise you that everything on **THE LIST** is designed to help YOU have a more joyful life in the long run (oh, and him too!). Remember, **THE LIST** was created based on what most men truly feel, way down deep in the darkest corners of their man-brain.

You don't have to do everything on **THE LIST** each and every day of your life. But the more you are willing to do, especially if it's from the heart, the more intimacy your man will warmly and happily give you.

Ready for the scoop? Okay, let's jump right into it. Enjoy!

## 1. Potty-time is private time

As far as your man knows, you do not poop. Nor do you let any kind of air, even if it's scented like roses, escape your backdoor. I know, that sounds nuts. Isn't there a children's book that reveals the secret that everyone poops? Let's have some reality here, right Jodi? Well, there's reality and then there's reality **with men**. They are two vastly different things.

I'd well imagine that the actions of your man's butt are something to which you'd rather be oblivious. Believe me when I say, as grossed out as we are by having to avoid the bathroom for 20 minutes when they finish in there, they are by far more sensitive when it comes to *our* poop (though they'd never admit it!).

When a man thinks of your butt, he usually thinks of smacking it while it's up in the air aimed at him or, for some unknown reason, actually getting in there with a vengeance. Men and butts—I'll never understand it, but such is the male mind, right? Regardless, men are fascinated with the female rump and it's up to us ladies to keep it a mystery—at least the icky parts of what it does when no one else is looking.

I once knew a girl (me), who for the first two years of her relationship (with my husband) would go to the grocery store down the street when "the urge" hit. I know! That's ridiculous! Alas, it is true. Of course, much to her chagrin, the damn store closed. WHAT WAS SHE GOING TO DO? Well, it took some time to plan her strategy, but she figured out when her man was typically busy or out of the house and tried to set an appointment with nature to only come a-knockin' during those times of day.

I realize that it can be difficult to time the natural actions of our butts to when our men aren't home or when they are too involved in a football game to care what we are doing, but there is a lot to be said about not being *too* comfortable with your man as it relates to your bathroom habits.

I once heard a husband, who'd been happily married for over 20 years, complain, "You KNOW you've been married too long when you are brushing your teeth and your wife comes in and takes a dump two feet from where you are standing. *I was brushing my teeth for God's sake!*" That story stuck in my mind like glue as it really said everything there is to say about how men feel about that fact that we even poop at all. I tell my husband that, "I'm a girl and we don't do that." He laughs and tells me it's okay if I use the bathroom like a normal person. I still insist that it doesn't happen…ever.

Sometimes, in any kind of relationship, there are things to keep to yourself. Pooping is one of them. While it's unrealistic to think you can escape doing it when he's home 100% of the time, it's certainly unnecessary to do it with the door open or to announce when you have to go. Mystery, ladies, is one of the keys to success with your man. You don't want him thinking of you as a poop-machine. You want him to long for your butt like it's made of nachos and beer.

There is but one exception to the no-poop rule: food poisoning or some other tummy illness. You simply cannot help it if you are sick and it's important to be able to ask for help from your man. Sometimes, you just need to hold someone's hand or have them bring in a fan to cool you off. Don't be afraid to ask him for help if you feel like you are passing a baby through you colon. Of course, by mutual agreement, that situation will NEVER be discussed again, by anyone, for any reason, EVER.

Just keep in mind that it's all the little mini-emotions that a man feels for us over the course of a day that shape his overall impression of us. While we all know the truth about what happens in a bathroom, the last thing we want to do is make our men recoil from images of us straining on the pot. Let him think fondly of your butt and when he sees it coming around the corner, he'll be more likely to give it a nice swat instead of running for the hills.

## 2. Act like your man is your hero, your knight on a steed, your Prince Charming, blah blah blah...

An easy way to make your man feel like a M.A.N. is to let him know that he is the big, strong, rescuing hero that little girls daydream about their entire lives. Yes, I know, today's modern woman doesn't need to be rescued, but, c'mon, there are things we like our men to do that make us feel girly. Guys are no different. They want to feel like you look at them as though they are Thor, God of Thunder. Even if your man is 5'3" and 110 pounds soaking wet, in your eyes he's a 6'5" Adonis. At least that's what he wants to believe.

Now, I'm not asking you to say, "Oh baby, you are so strong and manly and god-like," everyday. That would just be silly and transparent and eventually get boring. What you can do are things like these:

- Ask him to open a jar of pickles that you damn well know you could open. Then sweetly tell him that you love how strong he is. Don't make it a federal case, just a sweet comment in passing and then give him a kiss on the cheek or a pinch on the ass.

- Grab his bicep while you are doing something simple like watching TV or eating dinner and say something like, "Yum, yum, yummy! Baby, I love your biceps." If your man has the biceps of an 8-year-old girl, then pick another body part.

- Ask him about something mechanical, and then oooh and ahhh as he gives you the answer. You probably don't give a rat's ass, and you may already know the answer, but that's okay. It will make him feel good and manly to explain something "guy-like" to you.

The key is that this type of interaction shouldn't be perceived as overt or put-on. It should, at minimum, *sound* sincere (of course hoping that it IS sincere). The benefit to you is that when he does something nice, and you make him feel appreciated, he'll be encouraged to keep doing things for you because your positive reinforcement makes him feel good about himself—and you.

### 3. Compliment his one-eyed trouser snake

Men LOVE to think that they have the BIGGEST, BADDEST bouncy-stick on earth. Even if it makes you giggle when you look at it, act as though its very existence makes the world a better place. Why do you think guys like porn so much? The women make it seem like they'd just die without a taste of some guy's man meat.

Feeling desired by a woman turns a man on. Let's face it, it's a hell of a lot easier for a woman to get laid than it is for a man. We can go to the 7-11 and within 10 minutes find a guy that'll bang us. Women are used to being chased for sex a lot more than men are. Most men do not have that luxury; they usually have to work (and work *hard*) to get laid. Because of this, when you make them feel wanted, dare I say, lusted after, they will be more amorous towards you. Ironically, don't do it too much, as men love the chase—good grief men can be confusing! Ultimately, just keep in mind that when your man wants you, and feels like you want him too, he'll be far more apt do nice things for you in order to get your panties on the floor more often.

Now, some of you may be thinking, "Oh God, I don't want more sex, I want more intimacy!" Here's the thing, ladies…if your man feels cherished and desired, he'll likely be more romantic. Instead of his current idea of foreplay, which is probably something like this, "Hey baby, wanna do it?" (ugh, what a mess), maybe he'll remember what foreplay was like when you first started sleeping together. Just imagine—he might actually touch your boobs again or, (*gasp!*) kiss you before sex. What a novel idea!

Making him feel like his man part is the most glorious invention since chocolate and air conditioning is, at least, certainly worth a try. The payoff may be more than you ever dreamed it could be.

## 4. Try to avoid being a controlling lunatic

See, the problem with this one is that most of you who ARE controlling lunatics either won't admit to it or think that you *have* to control him to make the relationship work the way you want it to. So, I probably have a hostile audience on this, but ladies, bear with me. I promise not to lead you astray.

I can't express to you how many men lie to their woman on a regular basis because they would rather lie than deal with the fallout of being honest. This is NOT good for your relationship, (unless he's lying about how good you look in that hideous dress—that kind of lying is encouraged). You don't want your man thinking of you as either a dictator or his mommy. Neither role leads to a joyful relationship full of intimacy.

If your man feels like he has to tell you he's working late so that he can go shoot the front 9 at the golf course, this is not good. Why can't he just tell you he's going golfing? He wants to do something fun and relaxing...don't we all? Now, I understand if you have kids or you have no money or you have some other extenuating circumstance that might make you madder than hell that he's spending both the time and the $40 to go golfing, but it's important to balance daily responsibilities with day-to-day joy.

Let's explore the Freedom/Boundary method of non-controlling relationship happiness. You know that old expression, "If you love something, set it free. If it comes back to you, it was always yours. If it doesn't, it never was." What a crock of shit. Feeling free, even when in a relationship, is an incredibly healthy thing, but setting boundaries is also key to relationship success.

There's a lot that goes into this, so let's pull it apart piece by piece.

Freedom. Men, generally speaking, do not want to feel tied down. How do you think the expression "the old ball and chain" came into being? Really, does anyone like to feel tied down? We all like to feel as though our lives are a series of choices rather than a story written by someone else. Alas, there is reality though. You can't have total freedom and maintain a healthy, monogamous relationship. It would be anarchy! Men would be gone for days at a time and then show up covered in glitter, smelling like booze and loose women. We can't have that now, can we? Just kidding, I hope it wouldn't be that bad, but you get the idea. Just like children need to have boundaries, so do men (though they'd NEVER admit it, even if you held a lit match to their man parts).

Here are some things you can do to give him his freedom in a controlled environment (think YOUR house, where you can watch over him).

- Let him play video games, if he's into that. Men like to escape to a place where they are King of the World. Let him. It gives him time away from the pressures of work, family, etc... If he's a gaming junkie, then obviously you'll need to have some kind of talk with him (we'll address later on how to have "a talk" with your man), but if he just plays an hour a night and a few on the weekend, so what? He could be out banging hookers, so really, when you put it into perspective, it's not so bad.

- Who cares if there are socks on the floor or a dish in the sink? Remember, so much of a healthy relationship is picking your battles. Does a sink with a few dirty dishes really matter in the long run? When you are 70 years old and you think back on your life will you think, "Damn that man! He put dirty forks in the sink constantly. I don't know how I didn't end up burying him in the backyard." Of course not. If it won't be a big deal in the long run, don't make it a big deal now. I know this is hard for the ladies out there that are neat freaks, but it's time to give up a little control and focus on the things that really matter.

- If he wants to have his buddies over for the game, let him. Again, at least he's in the house. If you REALLY want to score some brownie points with your man, *encourage* him to have the guys over for the game, then make sandwiches and buy a 12 pack. This doesn't mean you are his maid, it means that he gets to brag to the guys about what a kick ass wife he has. I'll bet you 10 bucks none of "the guys'" wives would do that. Turn the game into your moment to shine!

Beyond his appreciation for you not being a controlling shrew, your man will likely be more kind and loving towards you because of your easy-going ways.

Now that we've talked about freedom, it's time to address those boundaries. Here's how you can make sure you get what you need too.

Let's expand on one of the scenarios I just presented. Try something like this, "Hey love, why don't you have the guys over for the football game? I'll even make sandwiches, get some snacks and buy the beer. And then after the game is over, you and I can snuggle and watch a movie or go out to dinner."

You may want to switch up the language of that conversation to better suit your own style, but you can see that you are both giving and getting in this situation. You get to be world's best wife AND get a nice evening of cuddle time. Believe me, most men will be so thrilled that you're willing to have his belching, ball-scratching friends in your house that they'll be happy to give you what you want once the game is over.

What you've essentially done by using this ploy is given him the freedom to hang with the boys, but you've also set a dinnertime limit on their stay without having to explicitly say, "But they have to be the hell out of here by 7:00." You've *implied* that they have to be out, so that you can enjoy dinner and a movie, but you haven't put it into so many words. It's those kind of subtleties (by that, I mean manipulation tactics) that will get you more of what you want.

The great part about giving your man freedom, while still setting boundaries, is that he won't feel smothered and harassed. He won't feel like he has to lie to you when he wants to do something fun because he knows you support him and want him to have an enjoyable life. When he's happy, you're happy.

## 5. Keep your muff issues to yourself

It's okay to talk to the girls about the rare, but horrifying, olfactory nightmare that is emanating from your nether regions, but as far as your man is concerned, your muff is a magical adventure land that every man on earth would die to get into. All he ever needs to know is that sometimes the *Closed for Business* sign is in the window. He doesn't need the details as to why.

Things to keep to yourself at all costs:

- Yeast infections
- Bacterial infections
- ANY kind of infection!
- Sweaty muff
- Period blood clots
- Soaking through your tampon and staining the car seat
- That not-so-fresh feeling of any sort

Remember, you expect him to occasionally put his face down there. Do you really want him to picture in his head what you yourself recoil from when girlie issues occur? Nooooooo! Believe me and every man I've ever spoken to, you don't want flashes of your not-so-healthy muff flashing in his mind's eye as you are having sex, or worse, as he's going down on you. If that happens, and his erection dies an awful death, then you'll wonder what the problem is and you **won't** want the real answer.

Visiting your muff should be as enjoyable as watching his favorite team win the Super Bowl, not as horrifying as his last root canal. Keep a little muff-mystery ladies. No need to share every last detail about your coochie. Let your girlie parts forever remain a mysterious, delicious dessert, even if you and I know the truth.

## 6. Let him relax when he gets home from work

Long talks and complaints can wait. Like Pavlov's dogs, if you train him to expect that coming home to you is a nightmare, guess what he won't want to do when he gets off work? Yep, you got it. Give him a reason to not only want to come home, but to long for it.

I knew a family that had a 60-minute rule: no one talks to Daddy for an hour after he gets home from work. Now, while that is a bit extreme, the point is that people (you are included here) often need time to detox when they get home from a hard day at the office. It's healthy to have a bit of down time before you get into the nitty gritty of family life.

I know you may be thinking, especially if you have kids, "Hey! That's NOT FAIR! Why do I get stuck dealing with the kids while he plays video games for an hour???" I completely understand that this is your gut reaction, but keep one very important thing in mind, you WANT him to WANT to come home to you. Period. There is nothing better than knowing your man is happy as he pulls into the driveway instead of thinking, "Oh, fuck me…what will it be today?" It's those kinds of thoughts that drive a huge wedge into a relationship. Let him have some time off when he gets home and then you can get into the necessities of the day.

PS: It's a great idea to always kiss him when either of you leave the house to go anywhere. Sending him off with a smile, and greeting him like you haven't seen him in a year will, believe it or not, give him the warm fuzzies, even if he never says so in so many words. We all want to feel loved and missed. Give him that feeling every day and you'll be amazed at how positively he'll respond to you. He may even start not needing a full hour of alone time when he gets home because he's so delighted to see you. Isn't that a wonderful thought?

## 7. Always remember that men are visual creatures

Don't shoot the messenger on this one! While on a personal level it goes completely against my grain to say this, it is the truth nonetheless. Men ARE visual creatures. They just are. And while that truly sucks in a lot of ways, we *can* use it to our advantage.

Always remember, men like hot chicks who give them sex. That's what they dream about at night and it's why they watch porn. I think that's not fair to us, because we can't always look like lingerie models and Lord knows our men probably have more hair growing out of their nose, ears and belly button than we EVER would have dreamed possible, but it's a fact that we have to deal with.

Whether you are a 5'10" raven-haired beauty or are 4'11" and as wide as you are tall, your man fell in love with YOU and who you are. Never forget that. You don't have to be some unattainably gorgeous freak of nature to capture your man's attention. All you really need to do is keep up with the little things that please your man's eye.

For example, I don't wear full face makeup on the weekends, but I do put a little concealer under my eyes and a touch of mascara on my lashes so that I don't look like the crypt keeper. It only takes 60 seconds, and just that subtle bit of makeup improves my face 100% without having to really do much.

Also, for those ladies that are getting older and a bit long in the boob (c'mon, you know it happens), buy those bra top t-shirts for when you want to lounge around the house but don't want to wear an uncomfortable bra. You can get them on sale at the end of the season at Victoria's Secret™. They are pretty and hold the girls up high. Men like perky boobs and while age may have stripped you of perkiness, a good bra top can make it appear like you have the boobs of a nubile teenager. A little misdirection is not always a bad thing!

In a perfect world I'd say that we shouldn't have to worry about such things. Our man should love us for who we are and that should be all that matters. But, in all honesty, it just isn't that way in most cases.

Some of you lucky ladies out there may have a man that wouldn't care if you could braid your underarm hair, and good for you if you do! Keep that man and never let him go. But for the rest of the ladies out there, just a little effort here and there can make all the difference in the way your man responds to you.

I know a woman who, once she hit her mid-40s, cut off all her beautiful strawberry blonde hair and gained 25 pounds. Well, dammit, if she wants to do that it should be her prerogative to do so. After all, we can't, nor should we, look 20 for the rest of our lives. There is something lovely about aging gracefully. Well, unfortunately, the result of her change was that her husband just slowly stopped romancing her. He didn't turn mean, he didn't tell her that her weight gain or pixie haircut turned him off. He dutifully kept that to himself. He just kind of fell away from her in subtle ways.

One day, while looking through a not-so-old photo album, she saw what she looked like only 2 years prior and began longing to look like that again. So, she lost 20 pounds and grew her hair longer. The result, you ask? He couldn't stay away from her. He started bringing home dinner (so what if it wasn't homemade, at least she didn't have to cook!). He started telling her how pretty she is. They even started having sex that lasted more than 2.5 seconds. It was like they were first dating all over again!

Ultimately, it's not about being perfect. It's about remembering how you loved looking pretty for him when you first started dating and doing your best to keep looking like you at least care what he thinks. We ensnare men with our feminine wiles; it makes sense that we can also keep them with those wiles as well. Just take 5 extra minutes a day and see what a world of difference it makes.

## 8. Try something new in the bedroom.

I scream and yell at men in my other book, *Sex: How to Get More of It*, to stop being so damn lazy in the bedroom. Now it's my turn to do the same thing here—though I promise to be slightly more gentle with you.

Both in and out of the bedroom, you get what you give. I sincerely believe that to be the truth. If, when you started dating him, you gave him blow jobs 5 nights a week and now you only do it on your anniversary...well...that could be a problem. I KNOW we all do sexual stuff in the early days and that after a few years we're like, "No way, no how, never again, get the hell off me." That's natural, because in the early days your man likely did all kinds of yummy stuff to your body that got you so turned on you'd have let him bang you on the hood of a car at the neighborhood block party.

But, if you've been together a while, in a lot of cases, that spark isn't burning quite as bright, so you lose the crazed abandon that once led you to do stuff you wouldn't even admit to your best friend. Add to that, if your man has totally forgotten that you have boobs or thinks grabbing the KY™ jelly is acceptable foreplay, my guess is that you aren't riled up enough to really do anything beyond the basics.

Here's the trouble with that...if he's lazy in the sack and you're lazy in the sack, for whatever reason, guess what won't be happening? Good sex will seem like a far away dream and you'll start to wonder if it was *ever* as good as your memory tells you it was.

Because of this, it's critical to not only make an effort, but make a big effort. It may kill your pride to do so. It may even feel forced or unnatural at first because it's been so long since your eyes happily rolled into the back of your head, but like all things, time and patience play a big part of success.

If you know he likes brunettes and you're a blonde, buy a long, dark-haired wig. If he likes spiked red pumps and a school girl outfit, go buy one. (Quick note here, buy naughty costumes online about a week after Halloween and then give your man a thrill once every 3-4 months. It's a cheap way to turn him on and rev up his sex drive as though you are 18 year olds in the backseat of a car.) Remember, healthy sex is critical to building intimacy and maintaining a loving relationship. I don't mean you have to have it 5 times a week, but when you do have it, it should be meaningful and delicious—not some rote behavior you do because you have to.

Not only does spicing up your sex life lead to better sex (duh...) but your man will be so damn happy that he's getting laid properly again, he WILL be kinder and more romantic. He'll want to do just about anything he can to keep the romance hot and heavy. You can even drop little hints like, "Oh honey...when you help me around the house it makes me want to do very naughty things to you." Talk about motivation! Your man will happily help you around the house if he knows he's going to get nookie. And if you are wondering, isn't that prostituting myself a bit? Maybe. But who cares? We all know that sex isn't just about sex. Sex is also about liking your man, liking how he makes you feel and liking the things he does for you. The more special you feel, the more amorous you'll be, and the same goes for him. It's a win/win situation for you both.

## 9. Be very clear about what pisses you off and what makes you happy

If you follow nothing else in this book, follow this one. Something I hear men bitch and whine about constantly is that they don't understand why we think they can read our minds. And I have to agree with them.

As women, we'll sometimes say or think, "Well, if he KNEW ME AT ALL, he'd know that would make me mad." Never believe for one minute that this is true. We like to *think* it's true. After all, we think we know our men well enough to often read their minds, why shouldn't they be able to read ours? The truth of the matter is that they can't. Women and men are wired differently. Men are often very obtuse and need to have things spelled out for them. I know that sounds just terrible, but we all know it's true. Because of this, you have to be very clear about what makes you happy and what makes you want to stab them in their sleep.

When I first began dating my husband, we had the "What pisses me off and what makes me happy" talk. That may sound crazy, but it was the best thing we ever did.

Here was my list:

- Don't go to strip clubs. If you do, you had better very convincingly lie to me or I'll kill you.

- Don't tell me what to do.

- Don't **ever** raise your voice at me.

- Don't check out other chicks when we are together. I'll go from sweet to bitch in 3 seconds flat.

- If you come home from work in a bad mood, tell me. Otherwise, I'll think it's something I did and it'll worry me and make me mad.

His list was far more concise:

- Don't be a controlling douche bag.

I laughed my ass off when he said that, but it was incredibly to the point and summed up exactly who he is and what he won't put up with.

That 5-minute conversation was the best 5 minutes I've ever spent. In the entire time we've been together, he's never violated anything on my list because I clearly explained how I would react if he did. And luckily, he doesn't want to hurt my feelings and because of that conversation he knows how to avoid doing so.

I even told him that I know I'm verging on insane by how much respect I demand when it comes to him not checking out other women, but it's who I am and he could either take it or leave it. Thank God he chose to take it. But had I not been *extremely clear*, who knows how many times I'd have been seething with hatred because he turned his head when a pretty girl walked by.

On the flip side, we also listed those things that make us happy.

My list:

- I like to be cuddled a lot.

- I like kisses in the morning.

- I don't like cooking, so feel free to cook all you want.

- I like chivalry.

- I like to feel like I'm important to you.

His list:

- Don't be a controlling douche bag.

Yes, I died laughing yet again. But for him, and for most men, it's just that simple. For us ladies, it's usually more complicated. That's why it's critical to TELL them what makes you happy or angry and to be totally honest about it, even if it's a little uncomfortable doing so. You simply cannot hold them accountable for behavior that they don't know will piss you off. WE may think that common sense would dictate what is considered good behavior, but we would be wrong. S.P.E.L.L. it out for the poor guy, THEN if he violates your list, let Hell rain down upon his head!

## 10. Quit saying, "Nothing" when asked, "What's wrong?"

I imagine that you are starting to get the point that communication is critical in a healthy relationship. We all know that, on a superficial level, but it really is the truth. If you can't be honest (most of the time) with your man, then your relationship will suffer.

As such, if your man asks you, "What's wrong?" don't say, "Nothing," unless nothing is actually wrong. Think of it this way, at least he's putting in the effort to ask you if something is the matter. He could just not ask and that would be far worse.

When he does ask, "What's wrong?" you may immediately think a whole host of things, like:

- How the hell do you NOT know? JERK!
- I don't wanna talk about it.
- Ugh, I'm not in the mood for a fight.
- How will he respond? Will he get mad at me if I say anything?
- If you weren't such an ass, nothing would BE wrong!

It makes sense that if you have any of those types of ideas running through your head that you might be tempted to say, "Nothing," and just avoid the whole thing, but doing that will not lead to a happy resolution.

When you care enough about yourself to realize that it's okay to be mad or sad and it's okay to share those emotions in a constructive (and brief) way, then you are much more likely to have a healthy, nurturing relationship. Unless your man is just a total jerk, chances are he **wants** you to be happy. Unhappy wife, unhappy life—we all know that to be true. So be honest with him when he asks that question.

And if you really do not want to get into it, or your mood is pissy because you are PMSing and you know you are overreacting, then you can say something like, "Honey, I know I'm not in the best mood right now. I just need a little time to work it out on my own and everything will be fine. If I need to talk about it, I'll let you know, I promise. Thanks for being so sweet, though. I really appreciate it."

By handling it like that, you've shown him that you appreciate him asking *and* you diffused the situation. If you just give him the Nothing Routine, then you are only postponing the inevitable. The longer that anger sits, the more it festers. There's no point putting it off if you know you'll eventually have to deal with it anyway. Just get it out there in the open, in a non-screaming, non-accusatory way. When your man learns that he can trust you to be honest, but in a non-psycho way, he'll be much more apt to be in-tune with your emotions, rather than trying to hide from them in fear of your reaction. It's amazing how free you'll feel when you learn to simply say what's going on in your heart and mind.

One last thought—men like to fix things, your problems included. If you give him the opportunity to fix something for you, he'll feel good about himself. You'll feel better because you got it off your chest and he'll feel like a hero. What a positive ending to an initially uncomfortable situation.

## 11. Your muff is not a weapon

Your muff is NOT a bargaining chip—at least not when used in a negative way. We women can be incredibly manipulative when we want to be. After all, it can be SO easy to manipulate a man with words or body parts because ultimately we know that men want that sweet spot between our legs. That body part has power, but with great power comes great responsibility.

Let's first address your muff as a reward; positive reinforcement for good behavior. I KNOW how bad that sounds, but women have been using, as my aunt always used to say, "Pussy Power," aka P-Power, since the dawn of time.

We're going to take off the gloves and get honest here. To an extent, we all use it that way, whether on a conscious level or not. Our man takes us to a nice dinner, washes our car, takes us on vacation...how do we typically reward him? Muff. Whether it's because we are in such a good mood because he did nice things for us or whether it's a subtle inducement to keep him doing nice things, doesn't really matter because it all leads back to the same thing: make me happy and my coochie is yours!

In reality, I don't think that there's anything wrong with that. Men have gone to war for access to girl parts, it's just a way of life. Where this P-Power starts to go awry is when we use it as punishment. It's one thing if your man has cheated on you and you just cannot tolerate the idea of having him anywhere near your sweet spot—that makes total sense.

But if you are not giving him sex because he pissed you off by dropping his socks on the floor, or he played an extra hour of video games during the week, then you are setting yourself up for future filled with animosity.

If you punish him with limited access, what starts out as the most cherished spot on your body will soon turn into, "What that bitch won't give me." If he can't get in your pants, even with a crowbar, because you are trying to teach him a lesson, that will likely only lead to a very unhappy, resentment-filled relationship.

Remember, we are trying to get you *more* intimacy with your man. If he's seething with rage, whether or not he shows it to you, he is not going to want to cuddle on the sofa or maul you with hugs. He's going to want to stay away from you either because he's angry or because being physically close to you makes him want to have sex and you won't give him sex, so he finds it too frustrating to snuggle up with you.

All of this doesn't mean that you aren't allowed to *not* be in the mood. Sexual energy ebbs and flows just like everything else on earth. There are times when you just don't want to have sex. When you are in one of those moods, one of the healthiest things you can do is tell your man so that he isn't wondering why sex went from once a week to once a month. Just be honest with him, in a kind and loving way. Maybe something like, "Baby, I love you so much. I'm really stressed right now and not in the sexiest mood. I just need a little time to get back on track and then everything will return to normal and you'll have to peel me off of you! You know I love your sexy self."

Ultimately, when your man thinks about your sex life, you always want him to have a stupid grin on his face. There should never be any negative feelings around such a precious part of your relationship. Using your girlie parts in a positive way can help ensure his happiness, your happiness and an overall happy relationship.

## 12. Turn off the bitch factor

I understand that we all have different personalities and different histories which have shaped who we are, but being a bitch for no reason is not usually an effective way to get more intimacy from your man. The rare man loves a bitchy woman, and if that suits your relationship, then skip to number 13. But, if you know you are bitchy and you know your man hates it, then take a step back and really evaluate the effects of your bitchiness.

If you find yourself snapping at him for either no reason or for the small stuff, take a moment and think about what snapping at him does.

- Does it resolve the problem? Probably not.
- Does it make him stop doing whatever he's doing that's pissing you off? Probably not.
- Does it help build intimacy in your relationship? Probably not.
- Does it annoy him and make him want to rebel against whatever you are saying? Probably.
- Does it turn him into a defensive jerk? Probably.
- Does it keep you at arm's length from one another? Probably.
- Does it make him want to forget he ever met you and run for the hills? Probably.

While sometimes we feel that bitchiness is the last option left for dealing with a man that *just will not listen to us*, know that it is also usually the least effective way of communicating with him.

Instead, take a moment, settle down and really think about what might work with your man. Sometimes you really do catch more flies with honey. If you are constantly annoyed with one another, you are not going to get the intimacy that you desire. Who wants to cuddle with a prickly pear?

## 13. Fulfill most of his "Woman Checklist"

In my corresponding book for men, I let them in on the secret that women rate their man on a point scale. It's all about how many points they earn in a given day or week that can earn them more or less sex and happiness. Unfortunately, men don't work on the point scale like women do. If only it was as easy as that. Yeah, sure, they keep track of stuff, but it's more like a checklist. A man's list is more like this:

1.  She gives me head.

2.  She lets me bang her.

3.  She looks good.

4.  She cooks.

5.  She cleans.

6.  She doesn't bitch at me all the time.

7.  She lets me hang with the boys.

8.  She doesn't nag me.

9.  She doesn't interrupt while the game is on.

10. She laughs at my jokes.

Now, I realize that list makes men look like Neanderthals, but on a base level, most of them are. We all know it's true. But, hopefully, your man also has a list that looks like this:

11. She's supportive and loving.

12. She's nice to me.

13. She's nice to my family.

14. She's funny.

15. She's smart.

16. She's strong.

17. She's independent.

18. She can Take Care of Business.


I know that you may look at those lists and think, "I'm not Super Woman! How in the hell am I supposed to do all of that AND cook, AND take care of the kids, AND go to work 10 hours a day?" You probably can't. Knowing what his list consists of doesn't mean you have to be the Perfect Woman (no one wants to live with her anyway) and cater to his every whim. The key is to identify what the most important things are to your man and to figure out which items you are willing to do.

For example, I don't cook. Maybe once a month I'll cook something, but I hate every bloody minute of it. If I had to cook everyday I'd hang myself from the grapefruit tree in the backyard. Luckily, my husband doesn't care. He likes to cook, so I'm off the hook. But, if without me stepping up to the plate we'd starve to death, I'd handle it like this. I'd go to one of those food preparation stores that'll make you tons of homemade food in large batches and then I'd put the food in the freezer. I AM willing to stick food prepared by others into the oven. Problem solved.

In most cases, there are ways to accommodate the items on the Guy List. Just try and prioritize what's most important to him and go from there. A happy man will do just about anything to induce you to keep fulfilling items on the list—isn't that ultimately what we are looking for?

*Make sure to read the *"Author's Note, Take Two"* at the end of the book for a little extra insight into how men really think.

## 14. Being a nag is a no-no

Nagging your man is one of the quickest ways to make him want to run screaming into traffic. Of course, if they'd just **do what we tell them**, there wouldn't be an issue, right?

Here's an excerpt from what I tell men we think about being turned into nags:

> *"Women HATE being nags. We hate it even more than you. Trust me. We only nag when you don't follow through on what you say; and really, that's not nagging—it's reminding.*
>
> *We feel like we've turned into our mothers when we have to ask you to do something over and over again. But sometimes shit needs to get done. If that's the case, DO IT. Putting it off doesn't mean you won't eventually have to do it anyway (the garbage can only sit around so long before it stinks), so just do it now and save the headache of her harping on you.*
>
> *Here's what a woman thinks when she has to ask you two, three or four times to do something you already said you would do:*
>
> - *That lazy fuck...why won't he do it?*
>
> - *Ugh, I have to ask AGAIN. What am I, a broken record?*
>
> - *Do I have to do EVERYTHING in this house?*
>
> - *WHY does he say he'll do something if he has no intention of doing it? Why doesn't he just say no? Then I could do it myself*

*or hire someone else to do it instead of waiting around forever!*

- *Are his video games, football games, and nose-picking adventures THAT much more important than me?"*

I'd venture to say that pretty much sums up how we feel about being forced to nag at our man. We don't like doing it. They don't like hearing it. So let's figure out a way to keep the nagging to a minimum.

First things first. Figure out how important the task you are asking him to do actually is. Will you die if he doesn't do it? Will your house go up in flames if it isn't done in the next hour? It's really all about prioritizing. If you know your man is indeed a lazy fuck, then you have to figure out ways of working around it. He is who he is and no amount of harping on him is going to change that. It's only going to cause annoyance, unhappiness and resentment. That is not the path to more intimacy.

Here are some things you can think about to help reduce both the need to nag him and the desire to kill him:

- Can you do it yourself?
- If you have kids, can they do it?
- Can you hire someone to do it?
- Does it really need to be done?
- What will happen if it doesn't get done?
- What is the real timeline necessary for it to get done?

These are all considerations to take to heart before asking him a 10th time to do something. Of course we all know that if he'd just *done it in the first place*, when he said he'd do it, that there wouldn't be an issue. Unfortunately, some men just won't step up until they are brow beaten into doing it. If that's your guy and nothing you say or do will change his behavior (because we all know most people don't really change), then you just need to figure out other options.

A lot of us have probably taken the route of, "Okay. If he won't lift a finger around here, neither will I." I'm guessing that was not a successful venture on your part. Your house probably just ended up a mess with half of the light bulbs burned out and piles of dirty clothes everywhere. Most men will live in filth and not even blink an eye.

Now, while I don't believe in having a "Saturday Chores Day" because we are not teenagers being assigned a To Do List by our parents, I do think that mapping out responsibilities isn't a bad idea. Don't get too much into the nitty gritty though. My husband and I have, over time, picked rooms in the house for which we are primarily responsible.

My rooms:

- The bedroom
- The master bath
- The walk-in closet
- The Mommy room (for visiting mommies)
- The dining room
- The living room
- The family room

His rooms:

- The kitchen

- The guest bathroom
- The garage
- Anything car related
- Anything outside

Additionally, he takes care of all the cooking, most of the grocery shopping, and fixes everything around the house (yeah, I know, I'm a lucky bitch—no two ways around it). Occasionally, we'll venture into each other's territory as a nice surprise. Talk about brownie points! It lets the other one know that even though it's not our "job" to do it, we did it anyway, just to be helpful. This is a great way to show love to your man and vice versa.

Now, if you think it's odd that my hubby has the kitchen, here's how it happened and it may be something you can do with your own man for various "chores" around the house.

When we first started living together, I'd clean the kitchen until you could eat off the floor. As my husband is a very messy chef, the cleaning process would take hours. I kid you not, within half a day it would be utterly trashed again. It DROVE ME FREAKIN' NUTS! All that work scrubbing the floor, sink, counters, cabinets, stove, walls, ceiling, etc... for nothing.

After about 6 months of this, I sat him down and said, "Honey, I can't clean the kitchen anymore. It takes me forever to clean it, then it's a nightmare within 5 minutes. It's making me resent you and making me not even want you to cook because I know what'll be waiting for me when you are finished."

Was that an easy conversation to have? No. Did it solve our problem? Yes. He is now the keeper of the kitchen. Keep in mind though, if the kitchen is a filthy wreck that I'd be embarrassed for my mom to see, I never complain. It's his room to worry about and so I never nag him about dishes in the sink. Since I've let go of control over that entire area, I can't have it both ways by refusing to clean it myself, but demanding that he does.

This is where picking one's battles comes into play. It's not worth it to me to have a perfect kitchen 100% of the time. In the end, when I'm dead and buried, will it have mattered? No. Then I don't sweat it now.

Do yourself and your man a favor and simply prioritize the "need to get done" vs. the "nice to get done." It will take an incredible amount of stress off both of you.

Oh, and always thank him for doing his "chores." Even if he doesn't thank you for doing yours. That kind of constant positive reinforcement will let him know you appreciate him. An appreciated man is happier and more likely to keep doing things for you because you make him feel so good after he does. Win/win.

## 15. Talking during the game is taboo

Just don't.

I was tempted to leave it at that, but here's the God's honest truth: unless the house is on fire, someone is actively dying in an adjoining room, or your need to give him a blow job has overwhelmed you to the point of obsession, he probably doesn't care a whit what is going on with you while the game is on. Terrible, isn't it!? Though true for a lot of men.

Let's do a little exercise. Think about the hottest guy on earth. The one you dream about or fantasize about while making love to your man (don't ever let your man know that though). Then imagine you get to meet that guy, alone, in the most romantic spot you can envision. He crosses the room, takes you by the hand, kisses you seductively on the corner of your mouth and leans in to whisper what you've always dreamt of him saying, and POOF!, your man interrupts you and asks you to get him a beer. DAMMIT! Now your fantasy is over. Your hot guy disappears. And you are left never hearing those magical words from Mr. Dream Guy. That's how men feel when you interrupt them during the game. Is that ridiculous??? Hell yeah! Unfortunately, it is also true in most cases.

Unless he's one of those guys who'd watch sports 24 hours a day and if you didn't talk to him during the game, he'd eventually forget your name, give him his Sunday football without interruption. He'll love you for it and that thankfulness will spill over into other aspects of your relationship.

And, so ya know, it's okay to point out to him that you are a saint while he watches the game—just in case he didn't notice on his own. Men can be a bit dim sometimes, so an *occasional* reminder of what a wonderful woman you are isn't a bad thing at all. Ultimately, if you let him have his man-time in peace, he'll be appreciative and show you that appreciation in the ways you want. Remember, the happier he is, the happier you are.

## 16. Stay the hell out of his phone and computer

Let's start this off with some warm, fuzzy quotes that back up my suggestion here.

> *"We're never so vulnerable than when we trust someone, but paradoxically, if we cannot trust, neither can we find love or joy."* —Walter Anders

> *"You may be deceived if you trust too much, but you will live in torment if you do not trust enough."* —Frank Crane

> *"When mistrust comes in, love goes out."* —Irish wisdom

> *"The best proof of love is trust."* —Dr. Joyce Brothers

> *"You must trust and believe in people or life becomes impossible."* —Anton Chekhov

Now let's get down to brass tacks.

> *"Ignorance is bliss."*

> *"Let sleeping dogs lie."*

> *"You can't put the toothpaste back in the tube."*

> *"Don't touch my shit!"*

I know, sometimes the temptation to dive into his computer's history and phone's call log is so overwhelming that it's like trying to diet in a Godiva chocolate shop—nearly impossible! Alas, it shows much wisdom on your part if you slowly back away from his stuff and allow him to have some privacy.

Believe me, I understand what it's like to desperately want to look into a man's phone or his computer to see what he's been up to. It's like a spider has crawled into your head and is digging its nasty little feet into your cushy brain until you cannot take another moment of it. You feel like you will go insane if you don't peek into his stuff and see what he's been doing. It can be like an obsession...an addiction that you are trying to deny. It's absolute hell. Especially, if you think something is going on that shouldn't be.

And then, if they just leave their phone lying around or their computer up and open, it's like they are inviting you to look.

They are NOT.

No matter how you look at it, they have a right to privacy, just like you.

It's like if your mom read your diary when you were 16. It would piss you off, hurt your feelings and you'd feel like you had no sanctuary and no one to trust. Your man will feel the same way if you read his diary (i.e.: the Internet history on his computer or the call log on his phone).

Now, if you are in some kind of hideous situation and he gave you crabs he caught from some skank, I understand if you root around in his private things so you can have ammunition as you head to the divorce lawyer. That makes sense to me. But if you are doing it because you are nosy or think something *may* be going on, you are better off not snooping.

Plus, if you get busted doing it, well...let's just say that will not be a fun day for you and then repairing the damage will be one heck of an uphill battle as now he'll think *you* aren't trustworthy.

We ALL have stuff we want to keep private. Whether it's a box of old love letters from an ex-boyfriend, emails to your best friend about how you haven't had good sex in 6 months, or the online Weight Watchers you're doing that you'd die if he found out about. We all have secrets. And that's okay. As long as those secrets don't fester and ruin your relationship, it's alright to have a piece of your life remain yours and only yours. Give him the same privilege.

## 17. Fight in a fair and constructive way

When a fight is over, it's over.

This may be one of the most difficult things to do, but it's also one of the most important. No one, including us ladies, likes to have things they've done in the past thrown in their face. It's not fair (I hate that expression, but it holds true here) to keep bringing things up time and time again when you are angry with your man. Let me assure you that when you say the following things, your man immediately either gets angry, defensive, offensive or tunes you out completely:

- Why do you always...
- Every time you...
- Remember 6 months ago when you...

Believe me, from the moment you utter those words, he'll be mad and worse yet, dismissive of everything you say from that point forward. Once a man is in this frame of mind there is no point to arguing with him because nothing you say will get through to him and the whole point of an argument is to try and resolve something. If, in his mind, he's thinking, "La la la la la...football, porn, video games, I wish she'd shut up..." while you are berating him for things he's done in the past, you aren't going to accomplish your goals.

So, how can you fight in a constructive way?

Here's a solution that works with most men. Yet again, it's about figuring out how and when to talk to a man. If you need to have "a talk," make it a bulleted list, not a screaming, crying dissertation. If he walks in the door from work and you launch into him (even if it is sorely deserved!), he's not going to want to deal with you. Or, even if you wait until he's had his first beer and is relaxed, if you come at him cursing and yelling and crying, you've already lost the argument. He may say tons of things to placate you (read that as: make you shut up), but ultimately, most things accomplished by a long, drawn out, weeping, yelling battle are only temporary solutions. What you want is a *real* solution. So, how do you get that?

While this may feel completely unnatural, especially when you are piping-hot mad and looking around for some sort of blunt object, try arguing like this and see how it works with your man.

1.  Ask him, "Honey, do you have a few minutes?"

    a.  Whatever you do, don't tack "To talk" onto the end of that sentence. That immediately puts a man on edge as they fear those two words more than prostate cancer.

    b.  By *asking* him if he has a few minutes, rather than *telling* him you need a few minutes, you're allowing him the opportunity to say yes or no. If he says no, then ask for a **specific** time when the two of you can chat.

2.  When you are both ready to start this conversation, take him somewhere private, other than the bedroom or the living room. Outside or the kitchen can be good places.

3. Once you've both sat down, reassure him that you love him and tell him that you want to discuss something with him.

4. Slowly, calmly and quietly explain what your concern is, without attacking him personally.

    a. "When you do X, I feel Y," is a great way to start. It's not accusatory, it's explanatory. And there is a HUGE difference between the two.

    b. For example:

        i. When you drink until you pass out, I feel worried and scared.

        ii. When you are short with me, I don't understand why and I start to wonder if there is more to it than you just being in a bad mood.

        iii. When you come home late from work without calling, I worry that something has happened to you.

5. Then let him talk. Let **him** fill in the silence. Don't feel the need to do that yourself. Allowing him time to think of his response is critical. Chances are you've been plotting this discussion for hours, days, weeks, etc...but he's just now hearing about it, so he may need a few minutes to figure out his answer. That's okay. Silence is okay. Plus, he's busy trying to think up his defense anyway, so any talking you do is falling on deaf ears.

6. When he does respond, listen to him, even if what he says is total bullshit. Give him a chance and then calmly explain your side of the story in greater detail.

But don't call him names or raise your voice or tell him he's a knuckle-dragging pig that you wish you'd never met (even though you may be DYING to say that!).

7. Once you've discussed what the issue is, end the discussion with "Thanks, baby, for listening to me. I really appreciate it," and then some kind of physical contact—a hug, a kiss, a held hand.

Now, I know you may be thinking, "ARE YOU CRAZY? I want to rip his nuts off and choke him to death with them! That bastard deserves to be drawn and quartered!" Believe me, I understand that urge. But this is all about how to have a healthier relationship with your man. If he dreads "the talk" or you yell, cry and call him names during "the talk" then he's going to do everything in his power to never have "the talk" with you again.

Unfortunately, him not wanting to suffer through "the talk" doesn't mean he'll necessarily stop doing the things that make you want to kill him. Instead it means he'll make "the talk" such a miserable experience for you that you'll stop wanting to even have them. Slamming the door of communication like that is one of the worst things you can do in a relationship.

It takes patience and practice to have an effective argument. There is a lot of trial and error, and as every man is different, you'll have to tailor your argument style to suit your man. Some men give in if you subtly guilt them. Some men give in if you are a solid boundary-drawer. Most men will listen if you just lay it out, in a verbal bulleted list without all the (what they perceive to be) "lady-drama."

It's important to know that this doesn't mean you aren't allowed to cry during an argument. Sometimes, you just can't help it. But be aware of how your man will react to your tears when deciding (if that's even possible) whether or not to show that kind of emotion. While there are many types of reactions men have to tears, I've identified a few of the main ones. Try and figure out which type of man you have and that'll help you know whether or not to really fight the urge to cry during an argument.

1. **The Placater:** This guy jumps right into "fix it" mode where he will say anything to make you stop crying. Unfortunately, what he says won't necessarily happen once the conversation is over. It's typically just a salve to get you to not cry anymore. He may even be well-intentioned in the moment, but quite often he's just grabbing at straws to stop the flow of tears and probably won't even remember half of what he said an hour later.

2. **The Deer in the Headlights**: This guy immediately shuts down and becomes a mute. Your tears terrify him and he has no idea how to deal with you, so he stops interacting completely. This type of communication shutdown keeps the conversation from moving forward even an inch, and then you have to try and recover from it and start all over again.

3. **The Jerky Prick**: This peach of a guy thinks, "GREAT! Here come the waterworks!" It may be that he sees your tears as manipulative and/or melodramatic, so he dismisses them automatically. When he dismisses your emotions like that, there is no way any continuation of the conversation will help you at all. (My suggestion is, if possible, to run from this type of

man as fast as you can. If he sees your true emotions and scoffs at them, he's probably a jerky prick in a lot of other areas as well. Why suffer the rest of your life with that???)

4. **The Self-Pitying Child**: This type of guy gets defensive as they perceive your tears as a personal attack on them or they feel so instantaneously guilty that their reaction becomes knee-jerk instead of calmly responsive. Once they start to sulk and give you that, "Yeah, I know, I'm horrible and I hate myself," routine, the real forward progress of your conversation has come to a screeching halt. They are too buried in feeling sorry for themselves to actually process anything you are saying.

5. **The Attentive Sweetie Pie**: A good and loving man will see that you are truly in pain and will want to really work through the issue with you. Your tears will be an indicator to him of just how deeply hurt or angry you are and he'll want nothing more than to resolve the issue with you. (God bless this type of man and I hope most of you ladies have this kind of guy.)

Regardless of which type of man you have, even if he's not listed here or is a combination of a few of them, just remember that your tears have power and if you cry wolf with them, they lose that power. Tears should always be a genuine display of emotion, not a manipulation tactic. When you are real and honest with your emotions, you set up an environment where it's safe for him to be real and honest too.

A final thought on this subject. While the Golden Rule of Communication is to treat others as you want to be treated, the Platinum Rule of Communication is to treat others as **THEY** want to be treated. Knowing that men are such different creatures from us, you have to keep in mind what is most effective in speaking with *them*. Keeping calm and rational may drive you crazy, especially when all you really want to do is hit him in the head with a cast-iron frying pan while weeping hysterically. In the end, however, it will help you better resolve your arguments (I prefer to think of them as "discussions") and isn't that the outcome you are hoping for?

## 18. Avoid asking him, "What are you thinking?"

Men have the inexplicable ability to actually...wait for it...think of NOTHING. They can literally sit there and have absolutely nothing in their brains. It's as though they received a temporary lobotomy and have turned into vacuous holes of man-flesh.

I know that we, as the more multi-tasking gender, cannot even fathom such a thing. At any given moment, we are juggling thoughts about the kids, work, the house, the family, the hubby, the groceries, the laundry, the state of the world, saving for the future, carpooling, working out, looking pretty, the bitch at the gym who always gives you dirty looks, how long it's been since you've had good sex, etc.... Good God, the list goes on FOREVER! It's impossible to imagine a moment in time where our brains are not filled to overflowing.

All you have to do is look into the eyes of most sleep-deprived women, who can't get their brains to shut off long enough to even sleep after a hard day of taking care of everyone but themselves, to know just how full our plates and minds are. Lucky for men, their brains work differently. This isn't to say men don't care about things or don't worry over stuff, but for some evil genetic reason that is utterly unfair to our gender, they can more easily shut it off for stretches of time.

This is why it's important to never ask, "What are you thinking?" First off, men hate it. Their first reaction, whether or not they say it aloud, is, "If I wanted you to know, I'd friggin' tell you!" Conversely, your man may be having one of those blank-stare moments when you could hear crickets chirping if you put your ear up to his slack jaw. In that case, if he tells you the truth and says, "Nothing," you are likely not going to believe it and do one of two things: either prod him for more information until he just makes something up (which you may or may not like to hear) or you'll stomp away in a huff thinking, "If only he'd share more with me." As you can easily see, neither one of those responses is particularly positive. So, why put yourself in that position?

I do have one exception to this rule and it's the only time it's kinda safe to pose that question. If you are having a serious, **relationship-altering** conversation and he's acting like he forgot how to make sounds with his mouth, then maybe you have to ask the dreaded question. Otherwise, don't.

A more successful approach may be to find a different way to ask the same question. Here are some examples of better ways to ask, "WHAT THE HELL ARE YOU THINKING?":

- Hey, Honey...you sure are quiet. (Then be quiet yourself and let him fill in the silence. If he doesn't, drop it.)
- Did you have a rough day at work? You're quieter than usual.
- Can I get you a beer, Sweetie? You are so quiet. If you need to talk about anything, you know I'm here.

With these examples, you are putting the ball into his court and being supportive at the same time. Let him come to you if he needs to talk. It keeps men from feeling mothered and hen-pecked if you just put it out there that you're around if he needs you. If you start allowing him to make choices about talking with you, instead of forcing him to, you are encouraging a much healthier communication environment. No one wants to be forced to answer questions they either don't want to answer or are not ready to answer. Give him time and space and let him determine the When.

Think of it this way—in 100 years, what will it matter if it took him an extra hour or an extra day to discuss something with you? Breathing room is one of the best gifts you can give your man (and one of the best he can give you too). So, when you feel the need to ask, "What are you thinking?" immediately turn around and stuff a sock in your mouth. That dirty sweat sock will taste much better than the response you'll likely get from your man if you hen peck him into answering you.

## 19. Live by the 10⁵ rule

What, you may ask, is the $10^5$ rule? This is how it breaks down. When something aggravates me I think to myself, "Am I still going to be mad about this in 10 minutes? 10 hours? 10 days? 10 months? 10 years?"

My reaction to the situation is determined by how long what is happening is going to affect me.

- 10 minutes? Sit and grumble and curse to yourself for a minute and then let it go. It's not worth the stress to harp on it.

- 10 hours? Maybe have a short (VERY short) conversation with the person who has made you mad, but keep it to less than 5 minutes, don't get riled up, and then let it go. If you won't care about it tomorrow, is it worth causing a fight that *might still bother you* tomorrow? Probably not.

- 10 days? It needs to be dealt with, but don't beat it to death. While not sweating the small stuff will likely give you a longer and healthier life, you do have to sweat some things. If you are still going to be pissed in 10 days, then you need to air your grievance and find a way to come to some sort of conclusion about it.

- 10 months? This is a real issue that could impact your overall happiness. If something annoys you today that will still be rubbing you the wrong way almost a year from now, then a serious discussion is necessary to iron it out and clear the air. This type of incident is not the kind to sweep under the rug. Doing so will only do further damage to you, to him and to your relationship.

- 10 years? This is likely one of those, "This needs to change or I'm going to have to do something drastic," types of conversations. This is another reason why it's so important to tell your man what makes you angry and what you consider to be deal-breakers. He has to KNOW not to do this kind of stuff or it's hard to hold him responsible for doing it (keeping common sense in mind, of course—you may never have explicitly told him not to bed your sister, but if he does, Hell hath no fury, right?).

Just like we talked about before, when learning how to have "talks" with your man, if you decide that what has happened is important enough to address, then it's important to broach the subject of your anger in a calm, timely, non-accusatory, non-defensive way.

If what has happened is so dramatic that it'll affect you for a year or ten years down the line, then give yourself some time to figure out how to respond. You don't have to fly into a rage immediately. You don't need to burst into sobs right in front of him. Sometimes, it is a great idea to step into another room and just process. Then you can cry or punch a wall or call him every name in the book while you are alone. Process the rage or hurt by yourself, and then come up with the most productive way of handling both him and the situation.

Yet again, it's about picking your battles. The 10-minute battles are usually not worth fighting about, so just let them roll off your back. Having that kind of attitude will save you from having a million fights about who forgot to buy the milk. All those tiny irritations just aren't worth the negative energy and the constant, underlying vibe of annoyance and disharmony. You'll find that when you and your man live in a home where you accept each other and don't pick over the small things, your home will be a warmer and more wonderful place to live for both of you. Ahhh...bliss...

## 20. If you are PMSing or having your girl-time, suck it up

Having your period sucks. No two ways about it. It's known as "the Curse" for a reason. We get bloated, hot, sweaty, bitchy, sad, and hungry. We can't sleep. Our backs hurt. We get cramps that have to rival a man getting kicked in the sack. None of our clothes fit. We have ridiculous hormones running through our body that we can't control. Plus, it's gross! Ewww...the things we have to do and see and smell during the whole adventure are simply disgusting. It's just a friggin' nightmare from which there is no relief.

And yet, men are shocked that we sometimes turn into bitches. If they had to go through that once a month for 40+ years, they might be bitchy too. They just don't understand, do they? They may empathize, but they don't understand. And because they don't, we have to figure out ways to not become psychotic raving lunatics during our girl-time.

I know, I know...easier said than done. But here's where some good old fashioned self-awareness comes in handy. Figure out what makes you want to kill him with a potato peeler and then try and avoid those things. Figure out what makes you a teeny bit happier and then *do* those things.

Let's take a peek at some examples of how you can mitigate your time while PMSing:

- If the mere sight of him makes you want to punch him in the face, then stay away from him as much as possible. Trust me, if you are a hormonal freak while you PMS, he'll be thrilled to get some alone time.

- If the way he smacks his food while chewing drives you to the edge of reason, don't eat with him.

- If you know that every little thing he does, including breathing, will set your teeth on edge, go read a book, watch a movie, enjoy some trash TV...in another room if possible. Go hang with the girls or lounge at your favorite coffee shop. There's no reason to be around him if doing so will only cause problems.

There's nothing wrong with simply explaining it to him either. While he doesn't need details about your actual girl parts during your PMS adventure or while you are On The Rag, he does need to understand how ungodly miserable you are. Just tell him, "Sweetie, I know I'm a big bag of crazy when I'm PMSing. I cannot help it. My hormones are running amuck, I'm in pain and no matter how hard I try, I'm just in hell. So as to not make you miserable too, I'm just going to keep to myself as much as possible. That way, you and I don't fight about bullshit things that wouldn't bother me if I wasn't PMSing. Sometimes, though, I may just need a hug and some quiet cuddle time on the sofa. How does all of that sound?"

While it may be a strange conversation to have, it does several things.

- It lets him know why you are behaving the way you are.

- It lets him know you are taking responsibility for how you act and that you are trying to figure out a way to make things go as smoothly as possible.

- It lets him know it's not his fault (though we are often dead sure that everything is his fault during that time of the month!).

By making him aware of both the problem and your proposed solution, you've taken the, "Holy shit, she's PMSing!" fear out of him.

I've said it a million times and I'll say it again, it's all about not being afraid to openly communicate your needs to him. If your man counts down the days to your girl-time every month because he knows a monster is about to reveal itself, then he's going to be on edge probably even more than you are. You can alleviate that by just putting your cards on the table. You may even find that after explaining it in calm, reassuring words, that he is more sympathetic to your plight and might even go out of his way to help you through it. That is certainly a great alternative to him hiding in the garage, biding his time and fearing for his life.

## To Sum It All Up

Ladies, first and foremost, thank you for bearing with me through all of the swearing, bluntness and honesty. Sometimes, it just works best if you let it all hang out, and that's what I've tried to do here. I've spent so many years collecting data on how men's minds work and I didn't want to leave anything out in an effort to be overly polite. I'd say I succeeded in at least that!

While I've given you 20 steps designed to garner you more intimacy with your man, essentially by being an open communicator and knowing how to "work it" so that he's happy as a pig in slop, there's one last idea I want to throw out to you: there is so much to be said for just being a sweetie pie to your man.

We know that men are freakish creatures from another planet in a lot of ways, but what does make them similar to us is that they like to be treated kindly. You, being sweet and attentive, can go a long way to securing more intimacy with your man. Everyone wants to feel the warm fuzzies in their heart when they think of their mate. So, give him the warm fuzzies.

Above and beyond what we've already discussed, here are some super easy things you can do to show your man how much he means to you:

- Send him at least one sweet text a day where you aren't asking him for anything—just a quick note to let him know how much you love him.

- Give him kisses in the morning when the alarm goes off.

- Bring home his favorite food or drink sometimes and then serve it to him.

- Go an entire day without adding to his "Honey-Do" list.

- Give him a compliment a day on any topic.

- Ask him out for movie night and let him pick the movie.

- Tell him you love him, at least twice a day.

- Serve him breakfast in bed once every few months.

- Figure out something he does that drives you crazy (socks on the floor, cap off the toothpaste...something not life-altering) and tell him you are going to let him off the hook for it. He will LOVE you for this!

- Initiate intimacy every once and a while...it'll make him feel loved and desired.

That list could go on for another 30 pages, but you get the idea. Being kind, thoughtful and loving are three of the greatest gifts you can give your man, and ultimately, yourself. Just being in a happy mood spreads joy to everyone around you. My ultimate goal for both of you is to experience happiness every day. I hope that some of the tips and tricks in this book help you find new ways to do that and that your relationship with your honey just gets better and better with each passing day.

**Good luck and tons of love!**

# Author's Note

A million thanks to my incredibly smart and
deliciously wicked friends who helped
get this book to its final edit.
Becky, Dom, Gina, Kathleen and Leo,
you are wonderful and I'll love you forever!


As always, thanks to mom for giving me a brain, gobs of
love and a strong voice with which to speak.


And thanks to my wonderful hubby, The Muffinator,
who supports me through my every endeavor.
I love you dearly.


Last, but certainly not least, a warm thanks to YOU, my
delightful readers!

I hope you enjoyed the book and that each day of your
future is filled with the blessings of a wonderful and
satisfying relationship.


**www.jodiambrose.com**

**www.jodiambroseblog.com**

**www.twitter.com/jodiambrose**

# Author's Note, Take Two

Ladies, I just had to share this with you as it made me laugh uproariously and it makes the perfect point regarding what men really think. Here's the back story…before the book was published, I had a bunch of male friends take a peek at it. It was important for me to make sure I hit all the highlights about what men truly want in a relationship. Below is the funniest bit of editing I've ever seen and I wanted to pass the giggles along to you. His commentary below is in **bold**.

### 13. Fulfill most of his "Woman Checklist"

*In my corresponding book for men, I let them in on the secret that women rate their man on a point scale. It's all about how many points they earn in a given day or week that can earn them more or less sex and happiness. Unfortunately, men don't work on the point scale like women do. If only it was as easy as that. Yeah, sure, they keep track of stuff, but it's more like a checklist. A man's list is more like this:*

1. *She gives me head.* **Yes**
2. *She lets me bang her.* **Doesn't matter if 1 is true**
3. *She looks good.* **Doesn't matter if 1 is true**
4. *She cooks.* **Doesn't matter if 1 is true**
5. *She cleans.* **Doesn't matter if 1 is true**
6. *She doesn't bitch at me all the time.* **Doesn't matter if 1 is true**

7. She lets me hang with the boys. **Doesn't matter if 1 is true**

8. She doesn't nag me. **Same as 6**

9. She doesn't interrupt while the game is on. **Same as 8**

10. She laughs at my jokes. **Where the hell did you come up with this one?**

Now, I realize that list makes men look like Neanderthals, but on a base level, most of them are. We all know it's true. But, hopefully, you have a man that also has a list that looks like this:

11. She's supportive and loving. **Still doesn't matter if 1 is true**

12. She's nice to me. **Doesn't matter if 1 is true**

13. She's nice to my family. **(Mother, not family) and still doesn't matter if 1 is true**

14. She's funny. **I don't even know how to respond to this**

15. She's smart. **About doing number 1**

16. She's strong. **NEVER**

17. She's independent. **Double NEVER**

18. She can Take Care of Business. **As it relates to number 1**

How's that for getting down to brass tacks? I hope you enjoyed his funny and rather sarcastic editing—it's always good to get a first-hand glimpse into the man-brain! Luck and love to you!

# Also by Jodi Ambrose

## Sex: How to Get More of It
A guy's roadmap to paradise, in and out of the bedroom

## Darn Good Eats:
The Cookbook for Creative Chefs and Reluctant Cooks

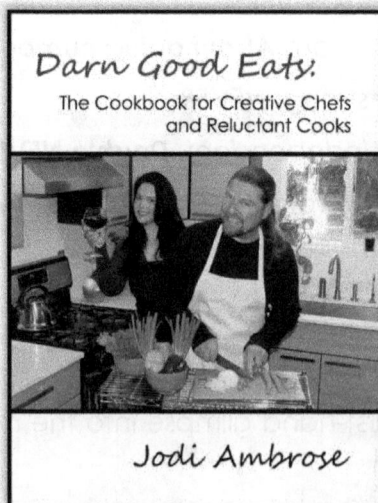

www.ingramcontent.com/pod-product-compliance
Lightning Source LLC
Chambersburg PA
CBHW060649030426
42337CB00017B/2530